HERBERT BI
MAGNIFICAT AND NUNC

GW01454327

Sir Alfred Herbert Brewer wrote his Canticles in D major at the end of a long and distinguished career. Variously organist at St Giles' Church and Exeter College, Oxford; Bristol Cathedral (for only a few weeks); St Michael's Church, Coventry; and Tonbridge School; he became organist of Gloucester Cathedral in 1896. The Canticles were premiered at the 1927 Hereford Three Choirs Festival, an institution with which the composer had a long association, having overseen eight festivals from the turn of the century.

Although now known chiefly for his sacred choral music (and this setting in particular), during his lifetime Brewer was equally popular for his secular music, including songs, and works for chorus and orchestra.

Published by
Novello & Company Limited.
14-15 Berners Street,
London W1T 3LJ, UK.

Exclusive Distributors:
Hal Leonard
7777 West Bluemound Road
Milwaukee, WI 53213
Email: info@halleonard.com

Hal Leonard Europe Limited
42 Wigmore Street
Marylebone, London, W1U 2RN
Email: info@halleonardeurope.com

Hal Leonard Australia Pty. Ltd.
4 Lentara Court
Cheltenham, Victoria, 3192 Australia
Email: info@halleonard.com.au

Order No. NOV291907
ISBN 978-1-84938-897-9

This book © 2011 Novello & Company Limited.

Edited by Jonathan Wikeley.
Notes by Thomas Lydon.

Printed in the EU.

www.chesternovello.com

NOVELLO & COMPANY LIMITED.

Magnificat and Nunc Dimittis

in D major

Magnificat

A. Herbert Brewer

Allegro ♩ = 66

SOPRANO

My soul doth mag-ni-fy the Lord,

ALTO

My soul doth mag-ni-fy the Lord,

TENOR

My soul doth mag-ni-fy the Lord,

BASS

My soul doth mag-ni-fy the Lord,

ORGAN

Allegro ♩ = 66

and my spi-rit hath re-joic-ed in God my Sa-viour.

and my spi-rit hath re-joic-ed in God my Sa-viour.

and my spi-rit hath re-joic-ed in God my Sa-viour. For

and my spi-rit hath re-joic-ed in God my Sa-viour. For

10
mp
For be - hold, from
mp
For be-hold, from
dim.
He hath re-gard-ed the low-li-ness of His hand maid-en.
mp
from
dim.
He hath re-gard-ed the low-li-ness of His hand maid-en.
mf
dim.
mp
15
hence-forth all ge-ne - ra-tions shall call me bless-ed.
f
For He that is migh-ty hath
hence-forth all ge-ne - ra-tions shall call me bless-ed.
f
For He that is migh-ty hath
hence - forth all ge-ne - ra-tions shall call me bless-ed.
f
For He that is migh-ty hath
mp
all ge-ne - ra-tions shall call me bless-ed.
f
For He that is migh-ty hath
f

poco rall. *p* *Slower*

mag - ni - fi - ed me, and ho - ly is His Name.

mag - ni - fi - ed me, and ho - ly is His Name.

mag - ni - fi - ed me,___ and ho - ly is His Name.

mag - ni - fi - ed me, and ho - ly is His Name.

Tempo primo *p* *cresc.*

And His mer - cy is on them that fear___ Him,___ through - out all

32
ge - ne - ra-tions. He hath
He hath shew-ed strength with His arm, He hath
He hath shew-ed strength with His arm,
f cresc.
mf
37
scat - ter-ed the proud in the i - ma - gi - na-tion of their hearts.
He hath scat-ter - ed the proud in the i - ma - gi-
scat - ter-ed the proud in the i - ma - gi - na-tion of their hearts.
He hath scat-ter - ed the proud in the i - ma - gi-
cresc.

Measure 42:

He hath put down the migh - ty from their seat,

-na - tion of their hearts. He hath put down the migh - ty from their seat,

He hath put down the migh - ty from their seat, and

-na - tion of their hearts. He hath put down the migh - ty from their seat, and

Measure 47:

He hath fill - ed the hun - gry with

hath ex - alt - ed the hum - ble and meek.

hath ex - alt - ed the hum - ble and meek.

6

good___ things, and the rich__ He hath sent emp - ty a - way

He re-

He re-

as He pro - mis -

as He

-mem-ber-ing His mer - cy hath holp-en His ser - vant Is-ra-el, as He

-mem-ber-ing His mer - cy hath holp-en His ser - vant Is-ra-el,

64
f
-ed to our fore - fa - thers, A - bra - ham and his
pro - mis - ed to our fore - fa - thers,
pro - mis-ed to our fore - fa - thers, A - bra - ham and his
mf cresc.
as He pro - mis - ed to our fore - fa - thers,
3
69
seed, for ev - - - - - er.
A - bra - ham and his seed, for ev - - - er.
seed, for ev - - - - - er.
A - bra - ham, and his seed, for ev - - - er.

Tempo primo (m. 75)

Glory be to the Father, and to the Son, and to the Holy Ghost;

As it was in the be-

85
f cresc.
is now, and ev - er shall be, world with - out
-gin - ning, world with - out
-gin - ning,
90
ff
poco rall.
end. A - - - - - - men.
world with - out end. A - - - men.
end. A - - - - - - men.
world with - out end. A - - - - men.

Nunc Dimittis

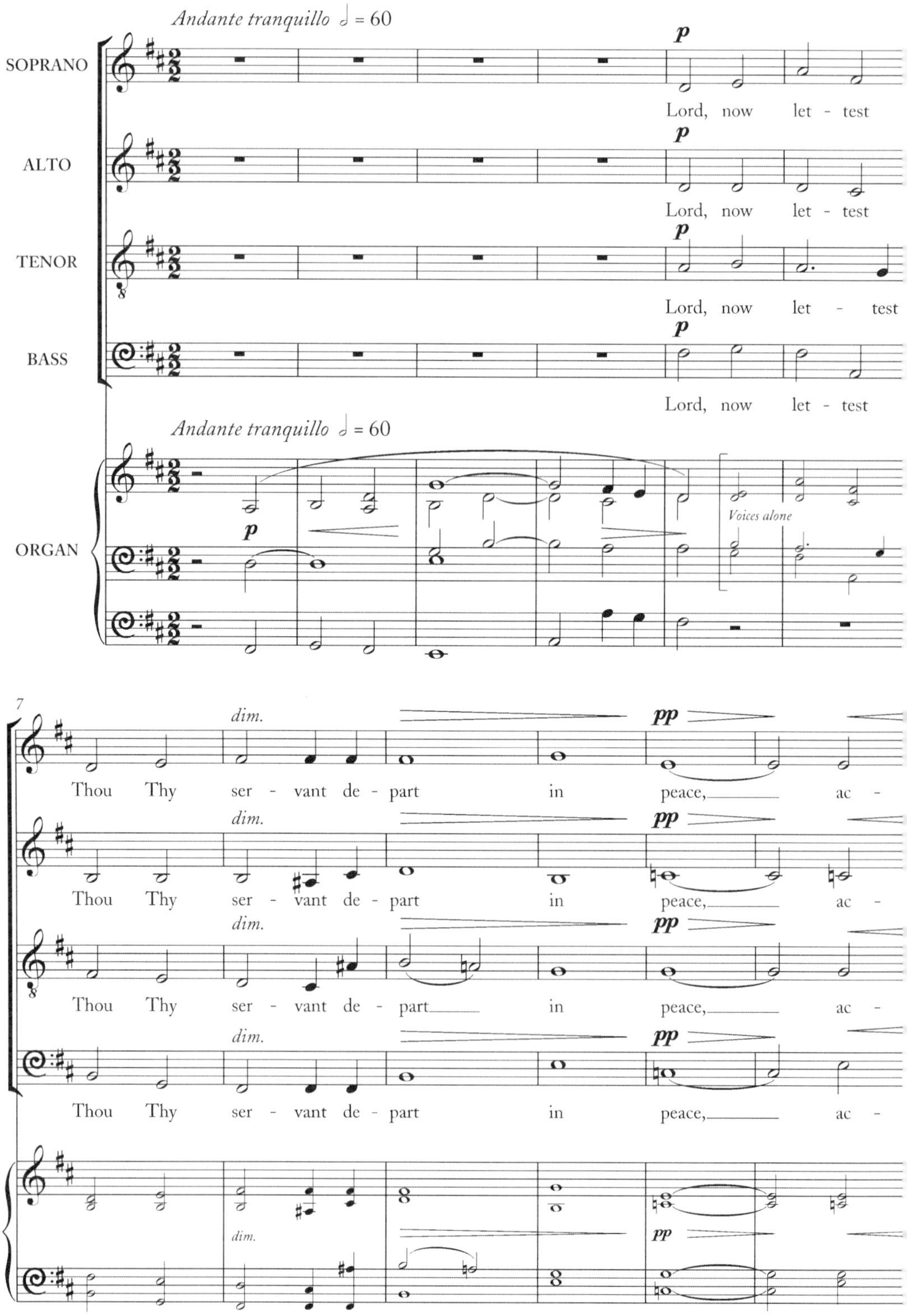

13
-cord - ing to Thy word.
-cord - ing to Thy word.
-cord - ing to Thy word.
-cord - ing to Thy word.
p
20
mp cresc.
For mine eyes have seen Thy sal - va - tion, Which
mp cresc.
Which
mp cresc.
For mine eyes have seen Thy sal - va - tion, Which
mp cresc.
Which
mp cresc.

Thou hast pre - par - ed_____ be-fore the face of all_____

Thou hast pre - par - ed_____ be-fore the face of all_____

Thou hast pre - par - ed_____ be-fore the face of all_____

Thou hast pre - par - ed_____ be-fore the face of all_____

Largamente

peo - ple;_____ To be a light_____ to light - en the

peo - ple;_____ To be a light_____ to light - en the

peo - ple;_____ To be a light_____ to light - en the

peo - ple;_____ To be a light_____ to light - en the

Largamente

38

Gen - tiles,_____ and to be the glo - - ry of Thy

Gen - tiles,_____ and to be the glo - - ry of Thy

Gen - tiles,_____ and to be the glo - - ry of Thy

Gen - tiles,_____ and to be the glo - - ry of Thy

43

Nobilmente

peo - ple Is - ra - el. Glo - ry be to the

peo - ple Is - ra - el. Glo - ry be to the

peo - ple Is - ra - el. Glo - ry be to the

peo - ple Is - ra - el. Glo - ry be to the

Nobilmente

Fa - ther, and to the Son, and to the Ho - ly

Fa - ther, and to the Son, and to the Ho - ly

Fa - ther, and to the Son, and to the Ho - ly

Fa - ther, and to the Son, and to the Ho - ly

cresc.

Ghost; As it was in the be - gin - ning, is

cresc.

Ghost; As it was in the be - gin - ning, is

cresc.

Ghost; As it was in the be - gin - ning, is

cresc.

Ghost; As it was in the be - gin - ning, is